PANGOLINS

by Jaclyn Jaycox

PEBBLE
a capstone imprint

Published by Pebble, an imprint of Capstone
1710 Roe Crest Drive, North Mankato, Minnesota 56003
capstonepub.com

Library of Congress Cataloging-in-Publication Data
Names: Jaycox, Jaclyn, 1983– author.
Title: Pangolins / by Jaclyn Jaycox.
Description: North Mankato, Minnesota : Pebble, [2022] | Series: Animals |
Includes bibliographical references and index. | Audience: Ages 5–8 |
Audience: Grades K–1 | Summary: "Pangolins' bodies are a rare sight. They
have scales and claws! Bright photos bring these unusual mammals to life.
Readers will follow along with easy-to-read text and will enjoy learning all
they can about pangolins."— Provided by publisher.
Identifiers: LCCN 2021029749 (print) | LCCN 2021029750 (ebook) | ISBN
9781663971753 (hardcover) | ISBN 9781666325638 (paperback) | ISBN
9781666325645 (pdf) | ISBN 9781666325669 (kindle edition)
Subjects: LCSH: Pangolins—Juvenile literature.
Classification: LCC QL737.P5 J39 2022 (print) | LCC QL737.P5 (ebook) |
DDC 599.3/1—dc23
LC record available at https://lccn.loc.gov/2021029749
LC ebook record available at https://lccn.loc.gov/2021029750

Image Credits
Alamy: George Philip, 7, Jiri Prochazka, 1, 9, 23, Mint Images Limited, 14,
Nature Picture Library, 12, roger allen, 28; Newscom: Photoshot/NHPA/
Anthony Bannister, 18, Photoshot/NHPA/Daryl Balfour, 24, ZUMA Press/
Afrianto Silalahl, 27; Shutterstock: Holly Auchincloss, 26, Joel Alves, 11,
Nick Greaves, 10, paula french, 13, Positive Snapshot, 21, Rich Lindie, 8, 17,
Vickey Chauhan, 5, Cover

Editorial Credits
Editors: Gena Chester and Abby Huff; Designer: Dina Her;
Media Researcher: Jo Miller; Production Specialist: Tori Abraham

Table of Contents

Words in **bold** are in the glossary.

Amazing Pangolins

A strange creature walks by. It has scales all over its body. It has long front claws. Is it a dinosaur? No, it's a pangolin!

Don't let the scales fool you. These animals are **mammals**. They breathe air. They give birth to live young. There are eight kinds of pangolins.

Where in the World

Four kinds are found in Africa. They are the white-bellied, black-bellied, giant, and ground pangolins. The other four live in Asia. They are the Chinese, Sunda, Indian, and Philippine pangolins.

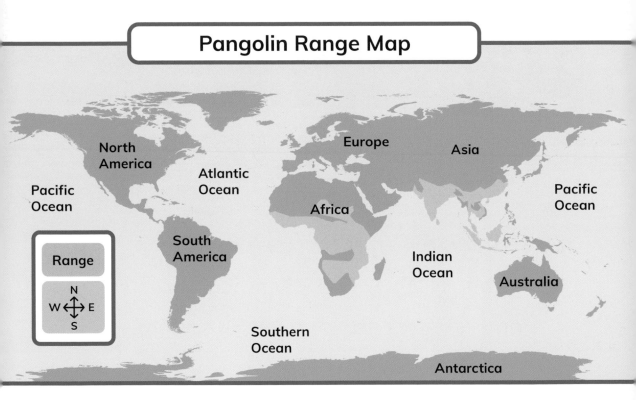

Pangolin Range Map

North America

Atlantic Ocean

Pacific Ocean

Europe

Asia

Africa

Pacific Ocean

South America

Range

N
W E
S

Indian Ocean

Australia

Southern Ocean

Antarctica

ground pangolin

Pangolins make homes in many **habitats**. They live in **tropical** forests and grasslands. They live in swamps and deserts too.

ground pangolin

Pangolins are **nocturnal**. They rest during the day. They are active at night. Many live on the ground. They sleep in large **burrows**. They may dig their own. Sometimes they use ones left by other animals.

Some pangolins are good climbers.
They live up in trees. They sleep there too.

white-bellied pangolin

Pangolin Bodies

Pangolins are special. No other mammal has scales from head to tail! The scales can be brown or olive green. They blend in with the ground and plants.

Pangolins roll up into a ball when in danger. Their scales are tough. They act like armor. They keep the animal safe from **predators**. Pangolins will also swing their tail. The sharp scales can hurt attackers.

giant pangolin

These critters are many sizes. The smallest is the black-bellied pangolin. It grows about 2.5 feet (0.8 meters) long. That's about the size of a big house cat. The largest is the giant pangolin. It can grow up to 6 feet (1.8 m) long.

Pangolins have long front claws. These are good for digging. They also help climb trees. But the claws can make it hard to walk. So pangolins will sometimes walk on their back legs. Their tails help them balance.

Pangolins have long and pointy faces. They have small eyes. Their tongues are very long. Most animals have tongues that start in the mouth. But a pangolin's tongue starts under the rib cage. It can be longer than the whole body!

On the Menu

The sun has set. A pangolin crawls out of its burrow. It's time for dinner!

Pangolins eat ants and termites. And they eat a lot! These animals eat up to 70 million **insects** each year.

Pangolins can't see well. They use their strong sense of smell to find **prey**. They sniff out ant and termite nests. They use their big claws to dig inside.

A pangolin digs for insects.

These animals don't have teeth.
Their long tongues reach into insect
nests. Insects stick to the tongue.
The pangolin pulls up the food.
It has special muscles in its mouth.
This keeps prey from crawling out.
It swallows the food whole.

Insects climb all over the pangolin
while it eats. To stay safe, pangolins
can close their nose and ears. This
keeps insects out.

Life of a Pangolin

Pangolins live alone. They only come together to **mate**. Females usually have one baby at a time. But some kinds may have two or three. Males don't help care for young.

Females make a nest in their burrow. They give birth there. Babies are very small. They are about 6 inches (15 centimeters) long. They are white. Their scales are soft. Over a few days, the scales harden. They turn brown.

a young Indian pangolin

The mother stays in the burrow with her baby. She keeps it warm. If danger is near, she curls up around the baby. This keeps the baby safe.

The baby drinks milk from its mother. After about a month, the baby is ready to leave the burrow. It starts to eat prey. But it still drinks milk for up to four months. The mother hunts for food. The baby rides on her tail.

Mothers care for young until they are adults. Then they go their own ways. Pangolins are adults when they are ready to mate. This takes about two years.

Scientists are not sure how long these animals live in the wild. Some pangolins cared for by humans have lived up to 20 years.

Dangers to Pangolins

Lions, leopards, and hyenas hunt pangolins. But humans are their biggest threat.

Scales that were being sold illegally

It's against the law to hunt pangolins. But people do it anyway. They are one of the most **illegally** caught animals in the world. People use their scales in medicines. They eat their meat.

The number of pangolins is going down. They are in danger of dying out. But people are working to help them.

Stronger laws are being passed against hunting. China no longer allows the scales to be used in medicines. Many groups are teaching others how important these amazing animals are.

Fast Facts

Name: pangolin

Habitat: tropical forests, grasslands, deserts, swamps

Where in the World: Asia, Africa

Food: ants, termites

Predators: lions, leopards, hyenas, humans

Life Span: unknown; up to 20 years in captivity

Glossary

burrow (BUHR-oh)—a hole or tunnel in the ground made or used by an animal

habitat (HAB-uh-tat)—where a plant or animal lives

illegally (ih-LEE-guh-lee)—done against the law

insect (IN-sekt)—a small animal with a hard outer shell, six legs, three body sections, and two antennae

mammal (MAM-uhl)—a warm–blooded animal that breathes air; mammals usually have hair or fur; females feed milk to their young

mate (MEYT)—to join with another to produce young

nocturnal (nok-TUR-nuhl)—active at night and resting during the day

predator (PRED-uh-tur)—an animal that hunts other animals for food

prey (PRAY)—an animal hunted by another animal for food

tropical (TROP-ih-kuhl)—having to do with the hot and wet areas near the equator

Read More

Hansen, Grace. *Pangolin*. Edina, MN: Abdo Kids, 2021.

Kline, Carol. *All About Asian Pangolins*. Hallandale, FL: Mitchell Lane Publishers, 2019.

Marsh, Laura. *Animal Armor*. Washington, D.C.: National Geographic, 2018.

Internet Sites

BBC Newsround: Pangolins
bbc.co.uk/newsround/37470783

National Geographic Kids: Pangolin
kids.nationalgeographic.com/animals/mammals/facts/pangolin

One Kind Planet: Pangolin
onekindplanet.org/animal/pangolin/

Index

About the Author

Jaclyn Jaycox is a children's book author and editor. She lives in southern Minnesota with her husband, two kids, and a spunky goldendoodle.